D0859574

	DATE DUE		

551.48   Conlon, Laura,
CON   Floods

64646

PROPERTY OF
SISKIYOU COUNTY
SCHOOLS LIBRARY

8/96 R13 9—

FLOODS

DISASTERS

Laura Conlon

PROPERTY OF
SISKIYOU COUNTY
SCHOOLS LIBRARY

The Rourke Corporation, Inc.
Vero Beach, Florida 32964

© 1993 The Rourke Corporation, Inc.

All rights reserved. No part of this book may be reproduced or utilized in any form or by any means, electronic or mechanical including photocopying, recording or by any information storage and retrieval system without permission in writing from the publisher.

Edited by Sandra A. Robinson

PHOTO CREDITS
© Frank Balthis: cover, p. 4; permission of Connecticut Historical Society: p. 7; © Kent and Donna Dannen: title page, p. 12, 15; courtesy of NASA: p. 8, 21; permission of Johnstown Area Heritage Association: p. 10, 13; © Lynn M. Stone: p. 17, 18

Library of Congress Cataloging-in-Publication Data

Conlon, Laura, 1959-
   Floods / by Laura Conlon.
   p. cm. — (Discovery library of disasters)
   Includes index.
   Summary: An introduction to floods, discussing their causes and disastrous effects, historic floods, prevention, and how to survive them.
   ISBN 0-86593-245-X
   1. Floods—Juvenile literature. [1. Floods.]
I. Title. II. Series.
GB1399.C66   1993
551.48'9—dc20   92-43122
                                                CIP
                                                AC
Printed in the USA

TABLE OF CONTENTS

FLOODS

Long ago, people built the first cities along rivers. The river provided water for drinking, cooking, washing, farming and transportation.

However, people found that river water can rise and spill over its banks in a flood. A flood happens when water flows onto land that is normally dry. A large flood can cause a major **disaster,** destroying towns and drowning people.

High, rushing floodwater can cause a major disaster

RIVER FLOODS

A river floods—spills over its banks—when it cannot carry away all the water that pours into it. Rain, for example, can cause a river to fill too quickly and spill onto dry land. Ice or mud, by blocking a river's passage, can cause flooding, too.

Flooding can also be caused by the melt, or thaw, of winter snow. Melting snow washes into rivers and streams that run into, or "feed," other rivers.

Hurricane rains in 1955 caused great damage along river towns in Connecticut

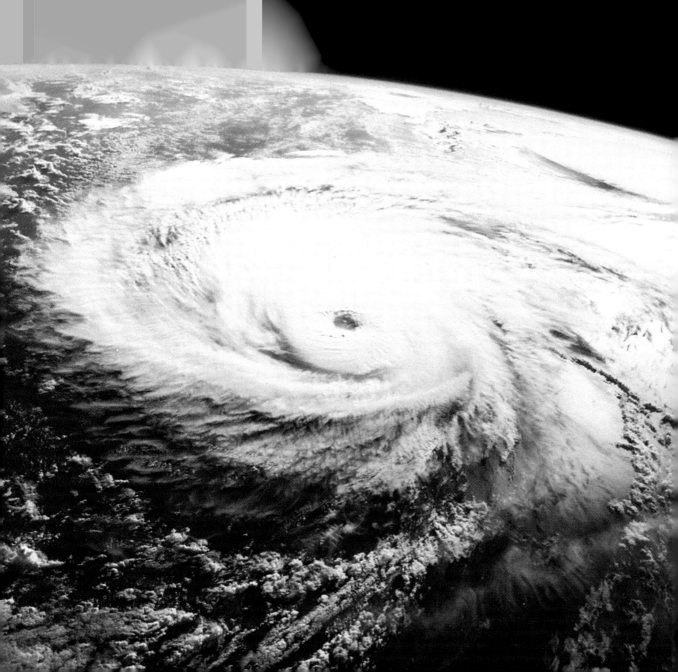

OCEAN FLOODS

Oceans, as well as rivers, can cause flood disasters. Undersea earthquakes and volcanoes can cause huge sea waves, called **tsunamis,** that damage coastal areas.

Hurricanes and vicious windstorms called cyclones can also stir up monster waves. Waves from a cyclone in Bangladesh killed 150,000 people in 1991. Ocean flooding from a 1970 cyclone in Pakistan killed 266,000 people.

This hurricane, photographed from a satellite, will dump tons of rain along its trail

FLOOD DISASTERS IN NORTH AMERICA

In the great Johnstown, Pennsylvania, Flood of 1889, a dam on the Little Conemaugh River burst. A 30-foot wall of water travelling 60 miles per hour smashed through Johnstown and killed over 2,000 people.

Heavy rains in 1927 caused flooding along the Mississippi River in seven states, and killed 313 people.

A hurricane in 1928 caused the overflow of Florida's Lake Okeechobee. Three hundred and fifty people died.

A broken dam let floodwater race through Johnstown, Pennsylvania, in 1889

Floods leave townspeople with huge cleanup problems

In Johnstown, Pennsylvania, the great Flood caused astonishing damage and loss of life

OTHER FLOODS

The Yellow River in China is called "China's Sorrow" for good reason. In 1887 the Yellow River flooded an area the size of New York State. Nearly 1,000,000 Chinese died.

Many ancient people told stories about a great flood that had covered a large part of the earth long ago. Jewish and Christian people recall the story of Noah in the Old Testament of the *Bible.* Noah, his family and hundreds of animals survived the flood on a huge ark.

Three people died and damage totalled $30 million when a dam broke above Estes Park, Colorado

FLOOD PLAINS

Egypt's Nile River widens and floods each year between June and September. It is a welcome flood. After the river returns to its normal width, the fields that it had flooded are left with a layer of rich soil the river had carried there. The low, level riverside lands that are flooded are called **flood plains.**

In many areas of the world, flood plains are the best farm lands. The lower Mississippi River has many rich flood plains.

Flood plains along rivers and streams make good farm land

PREVENTING FLOODS

One way to prevent river flooding is to build high riverbanks of earth, concrete or sandbags. These are called **levees,** and they keep high, rising water from leaving the river.

Dams also help control flooding. Dams are barriers that hold back water in a **reservoir,** a man-made lake.

Flooding is also controlled by digging a new channel, or river pathway, and rerouting a river into the new channel. A river flowing in a straight channel flows faster than one that winds around. It can handle more water, and isn't as likely to flood.

Ditches and canals help remove water quickly and prevent flooding

STUDYING FLOODS

Meteorologists are scientists who study weather. They help predict floods by using scientific instruments. Cameras in satellites show the location of storms. **Radar,** a system using sound waves to locate distant objects in the air, shows where rain is falling. **River gauges** keep records of a river's depth and show when it is reaching a flood level.

The National Weather Service is responsible for much of the information about weather and flooding in the United States. The National Weather Service has 13 River Forecast Centers to watch for flood conditions.

A NASA rocket carrying weather instruments blasts from its launching pad

PROTECTING PEOPLE FROM FLOODS

The National Weather Service provides flood warnings. During severe storms, people should listen for flood warnings.

Flash floods often give no warning. They occur suddenly—in a flash—after heavy rain or sudden snow thaws. Some bridges have flash flood alarms. When a river reaches a certain height, an alarm sounds.

Glossary

dam (DAM) — a barrier used to hold back flowing water

disaster (diz AS ter) — an event that causes a great loss of property and/or lives

flash flood (FLASH FLUHD) — a sudden flood following a heavy rain or snow thaw

flood plain (FLUHD PLANE) — along a river, the flat land which may be regularly flooded

levee (LEHV ee) — a structure built to raise a river's bank and prevent flooding

meteorologist (meet ee er AHL uh jist) — a scientist who studies weather

radar (RAY dar) — a system in which sound waves are used to locate distant objects in the air

reservoir (REHZ er vor) — a human-made lake in which water is stored

river gauge (RIV er GADJ) — an instrument which measures the height of a river

tsunami (soo NAH mee) — a huge wave caused by an undersea earthquake or volcano

INDEX